# House Music

Ellen Kaufman is a master of sight; her explorations encourage us to see the ordinary beauty in homely scenes. Unexpected grace exists everywhere, in the world of classical myth and in the modern beauty salon. Equally important for any poet worth her salt, she is also a master of sounds. She fills her poems with mouthwatering phrases like "dollops/ and fillips of tulips," and delicious appreciations of domestic details like the Singer sewing machine and Knabe piano, both of which have "names in gold/ on burnished black, both/ from an era of shapely/ machines that turned out// gavottes or French seams." Her sly and understated villanelle, "A Flemish Still Life," epitomizes Kaufman's ars poetica as well as her observational skill. "No effort's wasted if you aim to please," it begins. It ends with the gentle command "Aim to please." Kaufman and her poems aim to please, and succeed in doing so.

—Willard Spiegelman

I've been reading Ellen Kaufman's poetry for many years now. There's no other experience quite like it. Her language is taut and her aim unerring: her poems fly straight and true. Part of this has to do with technical mastery. She is a virtuoso of meter and rhyme, and her deep understanding of how structure works in a sonnet or a villanelle, for example, results in poems that combine pattern or repetition with an astonishingly singular vision.

—Jennifer Barber (full text in the foreword)

The intelligence behind Ellen Kaufman's wonderfully realized *House Music* is poised and observant, its reflections unfolding in sinuous sentences that are effortlessly elegant and deceptively plainspoken. The subjects and themes of her poems are various—the family romance, an encounter with a panhandler, the first moon landing—often taking the form of enigmatic vignettes and fables like "Sonatina" and "Thirteenth Night," pervaded by a sense of the fragile contingency of life. They pose the question, "Who can distinguish life from things?" and then answer it in the moving and masterful poem "Quilts: A Story."

*House Music* is a brilliant and powerful debut.
—John Koethe


Ellen Kaufman's distinguished poems achieve their purposes by modulating a powerful self-containment, a powerful and wise human awareness, by means of a chorus of exquisite and luxurious local effects. They are astonishing acts of balance, intelligence, precision, eloquence, vision, imagination, and grace.
—Vijay Seshadri

# House Music

POEMS BY
## Ellen Kaufman

ABLE MUSE PRESS

# Able Muse Press

www.ablemusepress.com

Printed in the United States of America

Library of Congress Control Number: 2013948808

ISBN 978-1-927409-25-1 (paperback)
ISBN 978-1-927409-26-8 (digital)

Cover image: "Girls at Piano" by Patrick Hamilton

Cover & book design by Alexander Pepple

Able Muse Press is an imprint of *Able Muse:* A Review of Poetry, Prose & Art—at www.ablemuse.com

Able Muse Press
467 Saratoga Avenue #602
San Jose, CA 95129

*For Thomas Merwin*

*Acknowledgments*

I am grateful to the editors of the following journals where many of these poems originally appeared, sometimes in earlier versions.

*Adirondack Review:* "Bank Story."

*Beloit Poetry Journal:* "Lethe."

*Carolina Quarterly:* "Anaphase," "Sonatina."

*The New Yorker:* "On Visiting Uncle Harry at Wingdale."

*Pool:* "Bonnet Contest," "Baton," "Donut Tank," "Waves."

*Poetry Northwest:* "On the Road from the Hospital," "The Walker."

*Salamander:* "Asters," "Raising an Orchid," "A Flemish Still Life," "Up All Night at the Tidal Inlet," "Emergency," "Looking for Silence," "The Portrait of Your Ancestor," "Return," "Thieves," "Waterfall," "Associated," "Conversation."

*Seneca Review:* "Memory," "Giraffes."

*Shenandoah:* "Cash Flow," "Fishermen."

*Southwest Review:* "These Lines Are Beams of Light" (winner, 2012 Morton Marr Poetry Prize).

*Tar River Poetry:* "Song."

*Think Journal:* "Lie."

In particular, I would like to thank Alex Pepple and Able Muse Press for turning this manuscript into a book, and Jennifer Barber for the introduction and feedback on an earlier version of the manuscript. Thanks to John Koethe, who chose "These Lines Are Beams of Light" for the Morton Marr Poetry Prize; and to Willard Spiegelman, *Southwest Review* editor, and Marilyn Klepak, benefactor of the prize. Thanks also to Peter Brown, Nick Samaras, and Vijay Seshadri for their support and good will.

Some of this work was completed at the MacDowell Colony, and I remain deeply grateful for the time I spent there.

"Emergency" is for Jon; "Song" is for Stephen.

I've been reading Ellen Kaufman's poetry for many years now. There's no other experience quite like it. Her language is taut and her aim unerring: her poems fly straight and true. Part of this has to do with technical mastery. She is a virtuoso of meter and rhyme, and her deep understanding of how structure works in a sonnet or a villanelle, for example, results in poems that combine pattern or repetition with an astonishingly singular vision. Part of it has to do with the way she counterbalances utterance with stillness: what she leaves unsaid in a poem is as important as what she says. I'm reminded of Cordelia in *King Lear.* Prompted by her father to put her affection for him into lavish words, as her plotting sisters have just done, Cordelia responds with a refusal born of love: "I cannot heave my heart into my mouth." The fuller the emotion, the fewer the words: a similar sense of restraint pervades *House Music,* and it is this that makes the poems so quietly but profoundly heartbreaking.

"Asters" describes the common purple flower usually relegated to "annotate the edges" of a garden. Asters, of course, have nowhere near the literary or symbolic résumé of a rose. Still, in Kaufman's portrayal, they are "wide-eyed and open-armed," as we might wish to be more often, as we are in our better moments. Their yellow centers hold "packed strands that stand/ for future asters" which is "a kind of meaning/ that might be minimized// except for the sheer/ expanse of it." Sheer expanse, sheer being: suddenly, the aster proves how vital—and extraordinary—the ordinary really is.

Because there is nothing that these poems take for granted, we have everything to learn from them. In "Emergency," a son's arrival home from school, "dragging his orange pack" is, in its own way, as miraculous as the day he was born, when, to measure his length, "nurses laid him flat/ on brown paper, and stretched him between two lines." Another memory surfaces, this time of September 11th:

> I remember, too, a red light impotent
> to halt a river flow of poppy strobes
> and sirens, neighbors huddled in singed air
> as lines of fire engines headed south.
> And how it felt impossible we should be
> still here, upright, untouched by fire. . . .

No collapsing towers are evoked, but by now we understand: it's as if this child dragging his backpack off the school bus bears the weight of all those who never made it home that day.

Each poem in *House Music,* in addition to rendering the reality around us, is implicitly or explicitly about the urge to render. In the expertly turned villanelle, "A Flemish Still Life," I love the way the reader becomes both the painter and the observer of the painting, and by extension, the poet and the one listening to the poet:

> No effort's wasted if you aim to please.
> Your pains are savored by the audience:
> a flask of cabernet, a round of cheese.
>
> The customer is charmed by what he sees
> and what is meant. All flesh is decadence,
> but nothing's wasted if you aim to please
>
> with oysters, lemons and a pair of these
> boiled lobster claws like bloodied implements
> framing the cabernet, the hunk of cheese. . . .

Immersed in the rich music of the lines, the deliciousness of the sounds, you might almost miss the "boiled lobster claws like bloodied implements," but that would be a mistake. Kaufman knows that being an artist necessarily involves some bloody-mindedness, a word the *American Heritage Dictionary* defines as "perversely cantankerous." The cantankerousness comes from seeing our own natures clearly, our hopes and failures and flaws. Which leads us back to heartbreak.

One of the last poems in *House Music* is called "Quilts: A Story." There's no separation between what we think and feel and the way we stitch, it seems to say, no other way to understand:

> The broken heart: yes, we know that quilt,
> worked in a series, over and over.
> It is made from pieces of potato sack
> and new velvet, thrift and squander,
> life and death, time within a border,
> which, used, eventually will disappear, washed
> into nothing, all work dismantling,
> a pink rag waving against the blue sky,
> pale flag of surrender, of having been.

Poetry collects the pieces; poetry assembles the quilt that attests simultaneously to our existence and our disappearance; poetry—so beautifully realized in this book—is the heirloom we need most.


—Jennifer Barber

# Contents

# II

# III

# House Music

I

# Waves

Permanent should be forever,
hair yielding to desire.

And desire should be this simple,
reshaped with chemicals and water,

smoothed by heated currents.
Florescent mermaids navigate

helmeted divers, neatly spaced.
Triton shakes his crown

of green plastic cylinders,
drifting between the mirrors

while blow dryers moan.
Combs in sequence stroke;

scissors flash like fish
as rollers fall, releasing flatness.

Incessant music pumps along
without climax or denouement

in the deep sea of self-admiration
which imparts grace to all motion.

# Donut Tank

We are inside it
without being in it:
the clockwise current,
the societal layers

of drift and stare
above oblivious coral.
Fish circle to the right,
vanish and reappear.

I find my favorite:
a purple-striated blimp
trailing a feathered streamer,
its ribbed, radial fin

translucent as lettuce.
We can't find it on
the identification key.
There is just one

that keeps arcing past
like a football lobbed
through a field of butterflies.
It becomes our game

to catch it lapping,
without effort, gangs
of angels and jacks,
triggers and parrots,

its idiosyncratic costume
a grape taste in my mouth,
its name something yet
to come, a kind of future.

# Giraffes

Told otherwise, I know they stretched their necks
reaching for fuller branches; now they're stuck
with appetites that won't return to earth,

the indignities of thirst. And camouflage,
that vanishing trick, is useless to prevent
fear or humiliation—see how they

kneel at the river, feeling vulnerable.
Better to play it safe and eat instead,
to nibble at mimosa; better yet

to ease the frail acacia from the thorn,
planting a wary eye on the horizon.
Then, in emergencies, there's time to fly:

legs can lash out in strides the length of houses,
hooves can strike like stones, melancholy
smiles can disappear in swells of dust

(her body lifting even as she licks
nervously at her calf, examining
as best she can, across that distance).

## Bonnet Contest

Beyond indifferent daffodils
and bleary cherries, dollops
and fillips of tulips

girding the garden,
the willows are willing
and poured.

Three giant rabbits
cower in boxes.
Three chocolate eggs

are lost in the planter
where Father has hidden
a tumbler of gin

and hollowed olives.
The whites of his eyes
are yellow like willow.

Pigeons almost choked
by double chins of desire
are diverted by crumbs.

Mother swills tea beneath tea
roses while the tiny martini
freshens itself, and there will

be a prize for their dark girl
with the peonies on her head,
stroking the soft fat rabbit.

## This Kind of Island

It's surrounded by blue
water that most of us can't use
for any coolness. You get
used to it. The screams are

for pleasure. Shrill chills
and thrills like roller coaster
noise—all for clear water
popping out of the ground.

And stopping. And waiting.
And waiting. And shooting
up all around and under them,
this one in his church clothes,

that one in her party dress.
Then the water pretends to forget.
Nothing. Nothing. Geysers!
Like a whole new city made of water.

# Dangerous Work

A cracked pedestal beneath the sky's noose,
the day so clear you can't see it coming.

Overhead an egret barrels through,
muscling from river to river, a white thought

like snow to plow. It's getting hot
under the earmuffs, the plastic hat.

Scaffolding rises like a blueprint
until we can see what you will mean

after your small part is forgotten.
We have our dogs to walk, we sense

the future. Some cross the street.
From there we can see more of you

and more you. Polka-dotted mixers
turn wet cement like batter as you

swivel on your platform, sun dazzling
that chain around your neck

dangling something. A cross or a medal.
A life's work in gold.

# Opus

To understand where I come from,
you'd have to watch my mother iron
white handkerchiefs with the radio on.
You'd have to put your hand inside
that zipper bag of cold damp fabric.
You'd have to see her inject
the iron with distilled water,
sink the plug into its two dark poles
and snap the cord onto a metal rod
to quiver with every stroke
like Bernstein conducting Mahler.
You'd have to watch her every week
for years and years. And then
you'd have to leave, trusting in
the steamy certainty of that job
while her leaden arm continued to
press a dwindling pile of old snow
against the silver surface of the board.
You'd have to know something
about the marriage of pride and scorn,
of scorch and starch, of perfection
and negation. And then
you'd have to forget.

## On Visiting Uncle Harry at Wingdale

Hungarian, our too-long faces stare
as if from mirrors or from photographs.
Austrian lines have written epitaphs
around Romanian mouths. Our eyes, our hair
speak Latvian as if they were born there,
while schizophrenic Uncle Harry laughs
at his twin knees, those sober Yugoslavs.
Our Russian bodies hold what they can bear:

trees from the broken forest, hearts of stone,
a loaf of bread cooling inside a towel,
or nothing, nothing much—a box of candy
packaged in some quaint Bavarian factory,
each secret kernel molded like a vowel
from every other language but our own.

# Anaphase

It began in the pool. I slipped apart
from the sloped bottom and knew I was on
my way to a blue suffocation, dragged,

at the last moment, back to a concrete edge,
where I found myself with a faulty sense
of balance, and the green world swayed

indecisively toward and away from the blue water.
So I disappeared for a moment:
first a child's slick head and arms

skimming the surface, breaking it,
then silence like an alarm. Silence
opening, after that, like a surprisingly large

body of water couched behind a curve, then
steady—the air conditioner's push, the audible
silence of summers; a pond by a pool

by a window from which a woman watches
her daughter learning to swim. The girl
is tense; the father is not to be trusted, letting

her go periodically, impatient to see her float
magically away. The mother, from behind
the window, thinks, tell her to breathe.

In another Olympic-sized pool, she bends over
absently, feeling her feet fly back, and the water
catch her unaware, and panicking, stands up.

How the mind heaves up its multifarious,
small embarrassments, at times like these.
How they speak in tongues, turning you into

the pillow, and out again, and meanwhile the quilt
has captured your knees, and you turn it off and turn
yourself to the flies' advantage. Better to decide

not to sleep, to adapt will to circumstance; better
to be able to dive right in, coming up smelling
if not like roses, at least of something distinct.

Better to stink. Better to pull the dead
of night full around you like a gift of time;
better to swim, better to dive, better to sink.

Yet imagine a road, as its dirt becomes soft
and soundless, and your legs are as part
of a cloud, and the houses recede in a slash

of sun, and you run as you sleep, and you sleep
as you run, and your breath is infallibly slow
and deep; for running can teach you

a rhythm; moving, a way to move. And so,
I can lose my feet. It's a beginning.

# Baton

Our legs stirred white pots.
Our tassels waved to brass.

Beside the horned goal posts,
cold metal burned

while turning.
The only true spin

was when it left the hand
for two heartbeats. The rest

a skirt of thumb and arm,
legs twirling a skirt.

They said the band played Souza.
You could have fooled me.

# Memory

Not a New England sort of wall
for which stones were plucked
from the earth like fat potatoes,

but remnants of the excavation,
each piece larger than a child, one
flat on top where I would sit,

smashing drab quartz lumps
into crystal fruit, sorting shades
that brightened in the rain.

Not a New England sort of house,
but the hard colors of a different zone:
azure or maize or chocolate brown,

children dribbling from the edges
of unfinished basements, one licking
spices from a sheet of wax paper.

And how the mothers drank
or starved themselves was still unsung;
a deer was dangled each November

like an early Christmas decoration
and when, finally, there was snow
unleashing a line of white beasts

behind the backyards, we slid
blindly down it on our bellies,
our lives hidden in plain sight.

# The Substitute

Her work came in the worst of weather,
sleet pricking the windshield,
gusts breaching the seams
of the convertible top that was held together

with silver duct tape and stripe of air.
The car idled and filled with smoke,
the Camel pressed by her bright lips
a miniature of the tailpipe that blew fire

into the banked perimeter of snow.
The laziest of students, we endured
a frigid back-seat wait to cop a ride
uphill, behind the plow

where sprays of blindness would undo
our stifled giggles like a girdle.
At school she'd reappear,
teacher of anything but what she knew,

which was how, simply, to survive
by never seeing things as others did.
She rubbed a clearing in the windshield
large enough so she could drive;

the view viewed from *reverse*
gave us the center of her living room:
an abstract oil by her dead husband
like summer staring back at us.

# Apollo 11

The moon is so lit
I can almost see Neil Armstrong
bouncing in white dust
forty years ago,

Buzz Aldrin dropping down beside him,
and Collins still in orbit.
Wherever we were that day,
we were also on the moon,

six times lighter
in the late sixties,
their voices crackling
back to us in time delay

across the "magnificent desolation"
as coined by Aldrin.
In a cabin in New Hampshire,
I was peeling off

my slick green Speedo
to Armstrong's giant leap
instead of the usual
"Light My Fire" or bulletins

of rioting and war
beamed in from Boston.
There was a way to be modest
with the other girls

inside a towel.
It was the summer of '69
and the moon had lost her virginity.
Men danced on her.

## Cash Flow

Those twenty dollars missing from your wallet
remind you of the moment when you slipped
them in your wallet, thinking of something
else. These are the absent moments.
You touch yourself for hints of reassurance:
no wallet! Blood rushes from your face.
You find it though—it's in a different pocket.
A narrow brush. These are the precious moments.
A blind panhandler taps you on the shoulder.
Absently, you pull your wallet from your
pocket, comb yourself for change. He thanks
you very much. He taps you on the shoulder,
hands you back your twenty dollars. Blood
rushes to your face. You thank him very much.
These were the missing moments. All is well
until he taps you on the shoulder, hands you back
your wallet. Blood rushes to your face. A close
escape. You thank him very much. Arriving home,
you're missing twenty dollars. You comb your wallet.
You can't remember. Blood rushes from your face
and fills your pockets. These are the narrow moments.

# Waterfall

Everyone's snapshots will go into the same
album. No captions will explain the falling
water. Whether she's the daughter or the wife.
The skin colors. What they did all
day. Group by group, they pose against
the water. It drowns out Seventh
Avenue. Puddles in the vinyl seat cushions keep
them moving. A few green umbrellas have been
opened; checkered sunlight filters down behind the honey
locusts, blackening their slim, dark
stems. A cop on foot with no place else to
be pauses next to a barrel of pink
impatiens. One instant replaces the next so
slowly you can see how it works.

# Rayos X

Radiology is underground.
The technician, a large woman,
marks my nipples and scars
with tiny flowered Band-Aids,

apologizes for the glass
plate that pins my shoulder
blade. Some say it hurts.
Above us, stories of births

and deaths rise up, closed eyes
and pulsing lips, each brain
tuned to a different channel.
An infant latches to a bottle

as my breast fills the screen
like a slab of marble.
The image is reversible,
but not the truth.

Technology is smart,
always improving itself,
but cancer is a bad student,
repeating the same mistake

like the bold and the beautiful
on the waiting room TV,
their endless stories flickering
in the cave's false brightness.

## The sewing machine & the piano

wore their names in gold
on burnished black, both
from an era of shapely
machines that turned out

gavottes or French seams,
practice finishing the raw
edges into a smoothness
young hands learned to fashion

from hammers or a needle.
Later, the equipment seemed
too much for the occasional need:
a hem, a tune, the mastered

slowly unraveling, and so
they passed them on to me,
one from each sister, a Knabe
and a Singer. Both sang,

but one needed an electrician
and the other a technician.
Both had possibilities
beyond my abilities,

and temperaments that needed
either oil or a dry climate.
An instruction booklet
referred to missing attachments.

Even so, I relearned how to sew
and, as for the piano, my stiff
fingers still knew how to read.
I plowed through children's pieces

just to hear them again,
trilled clumsily in slow motion.
What did I make? Halting lines
in counterpoint, a broken line

that underneath held tight—
over and over and over.

## Asters

Wide-eyed and open-armed,
they annotate the edges

with stars leading nowhere.
Stuck with the same

purple, they repeat themselves.
Their yellow centers

are packed strands that stand
for future asters.

It's a kind of meaning
that might be minimized

except for the sheer
expanse of it.

II

# Up All Night at the Tidal Inlet

A fine stink when the tide goes out:
all that false blue turned to brown,
stooped figures in dark waders
clawing mud in the slant sun,

then hauling buckets to the parking lot.
The pretty sails are farther down
where water still separates the shores,
where the sunset is happening.

Up here, it's smoky between the fires,
Grandma passing out cigarettes and gin,
Crystal finding a better station,
baby juicing, the little boy dancing

to whatever she wants to hear.
We zip into our tent, our sleeping bags.
Dead branches slide by our heads
and take the ax, kindling crackles

until our insides light: *motherfucker!*
Crystal in tears now turning the dial
to where it stops. It gets no louder.

At five the baby cries, but no one answers.
You know the tide is in
when salt fills your nose.

# Suspension Bridge

Man overboard:
silence and then a crack
as water mimics rock.
Who pulls the cord,

invisible, yet strong
enough to surface him
like glass through skin?
Up again, hammering

hands with buddies—
a boy, yet older
and solid as a soldier,
T-shirt and Levis

stuck to his frame,
he's a licked cigarette.
Again. He legs his wet
desire double-time

over the wooden rail,
eyes tracing the known
descent, forty feet down
into dappled steel,

then steps into air,
body at attention
to minimize friction.
It feels like forever.

# Fishermen

It is easy for them to wait; it is
the nature of the sport, and it
   is in their nature.
A deceiving thing—the casting out
   and reeling in—
of motionless motion, a figure
of the ocean, a trust.
   Have you been taken in?
At dusk the light escapes
   around the edges of day, and takes
with it rod and line, the fine
division of the sea and sky,
   and fishermen
are lined up along the shore
   like boys at a urinal. A rich
and vacant mood hangs in the air
like air. The fish, perhaps,
   are feeding here
and there. Would you be taken in?

# Bank Story

The river needed more room,
and so it took a room
for itself along the water's edge,

lolled porch-side in the downpour,
came up against the curved road
with its own proposal drowning out

theirs, until the river was a road
and the road a river
spreading through windows

like a liquid view, trees wavering
on the surface amid clouds
and, after all, the dilatory sun

drying the paper bedrooms and
the rusted kitchen until, finally,
the crooked house returned

and the river, again homeless,
was back in its old place between
the banks, washing itself on rocks.

## Contra Dance

You say we could be happy in the country.
I step out of my life to try it out.

I bend to touch the cat as she runs in
with something in her mouth. Then you come out

in country clothes, your shirt canary yellow
with big white letters spelling where we live.

The screen door slams. It's me this time,
dumping an armful of greens into the sink

while you are yelling through the window. What,
I cry, the water spilling gently through

my hands. Come out, you say, and see the country.
The country's very beautiful out here.

You wave, up to your waist in blackberries.
Lugging the giant clippers, I step out.

# Sonatina

What space between us and the sky amazes
sometimes. The clouds thin out
against the moon. We watch them slide,

drawn by some wind that hasn't settled here.
Down here it's still, the cars so far away
they sound like ocean. This could be the woods,

this backyard lawn a clearing with the house
hunched up in shadow like a bluff. But a bird
rummages through the rosebush, petals fall

on what we know to be a lawn, on our
impoverished example of a lawn.
The crabgrass pokes our arms as we lie back,

arm beside arm, looking up at distance,
imagining the speed of light drawn back
to stars. Impatiently, as if to jar us,

our neighbor's car swings open and starts up:
leather upholstery and electric overdrive,
a space machine for rutted country roads

soon to be stalled for hours in the lot
of the country-western bar on Route 13,
we think, because we saw him there one night

dancing too slowly with the owner's wife.
Another door kicks open in my mind:
a chilly scene discovered as by me,

though we were in it like a still life,
our arms and legs gleaming like wire hangers
tangled in the bottom of a closet,

and a third figure standing in the door
as if imagined. The door slams shut;
the Corvette revs, spits gravel through the shrubs

and vanishes. The stars again, cicadas.
A light comes on, familiar shapes retreat:
our friendly neighbors, on the other side,

home from the movies after twenty years
of coming home together to this parlor
of calico upholstery and plants.

The room is neat and cluttered all at once,
relics pinned up or tucked away in corners,
the lampshade gently rocking in the window.

Our lawn is gullied by a stream of light,
our night by soft TV. The liquid stars
are tears. The flat earth sways when someone

slams the door. We can't believe we're even
here, but look how comfortable we've tried
to make it: white roses and blue pillows.

# Thirteenth Night

*Delacorte Theater, Central Park*

Virtuous Olivia, oblivious
to Orsino's advances, is
mournfully attired
in a black-tiered
gown that presages

her body's urge
to slip that cage
and fall for the pretty twin
sister of Sebastian,
disguised as a page.

The body has its will
in phases palatable
to the mind.
The mind, in kind,
yields to a counter spell

cast by the body. Soon,
night falls. The rain
waits in the wings
while the fool sings.
From bushes green,

a masked varmint enters
behind the characters.
Open to the elements,
a stage admits to chance
as a ship harbors

mice and players submit
to mysteries of plot,
whatever weird
or wonderful. Appeared,
now it must not

be questioned, like the sea
or the moon's eye
in it. Torn parts cast
away, like sail and mast,
magically rejoin in comedy,

halves to their missing halves.
The beast withdraws
(music being food,
but food also being food)
to darker passages.

# On the Road from the Hospital

The institutions start to rub off on you—
the hospital won't stay put, its adjunct
rescue squad flipping through back roads.
The schoolteacher reeks of school, her trunk

of paperbacks spilled over the snow, one
long white braid twitching at her waist.
Back at the hospital, your mother dozed
through her black mood, woke

to refuse another meal and smile at us—
everything frozen in the state of not
dead yet, which, of course, is life:
a dull, slick glaze across the road

to leave on, one day, as visitors
and return on as patients—astonishing
or not, a familiar story. Inexperienced,
you can't believe in cancer, then can't

believe in cures. Bumper cars. A Buick
sliding toward you like trick photography.
The shutter explodes. The road reverses
itself. We lie, bruised, side by side

in the ambulance, all right really, able
to answer the questions. Colliding cells
on glass. Saved by a seat belt. It was
her fault. It could happen to anyone.

# A Rest Stop in Connecticut

Cruise in with *Graceland* pumping,
silver-headed men filling their silver cars
while you idle, emptying yours.

Gas is up again. Or is it down?
Children skip past *you are here*
on the giant glass-enclosed map

edged with sails and fishes.
This ocean smells like gasoline.
*I don't want no more of your crazy love*

stops at *crazy* when you turn the key.
Filled, now park and disembark
to rest from being at rest,

toilets a predictable disaster.
Dogs must remain on leash
and coffee costs the same

for small, medium or large:
today's economic conundrum.
Beyond fenced-in grass,

a slow stream nuzzles trash.
The expressway hisses like surf,
pretending not to change.

## Associated

The five-and-ten is now a supermarket.
Florescence jounces off the white walls
like thoughts in a mind without memory.

New tight aisles of sweet and brine:
even this mild, convenient change
is disconcerting, a reminder that you're gone.

The interminable winter you spent
tagging all of your possessions,
labeling them with our names,

is over. Now we live without you
among the merchandise.
Now when I lose myself in some

tedious chore I've learned to like
—now, sewing on this button—
I think of you, tying cakes of soap

onto your tiny new pear trees
to keep the deer away. I see
the pear trees, but I can't see you.

I see the deer. I see my name
lettered in one neat block, tied
to the handlebar of your old Schwinn.

## Class of '73

In the parking lot,
*Got any pot?*

Adult laughter
and smiles thereafter:

not even a cigarette
or any bad habit

besides duplicity
beclouds the day.

Each of us is two,
the old and the new,

as we pass into the unrecognizable
yet remembered school

that has ripened with time
and money, a tame

penetration of bodies
into Saturday emptiness.

No straw wrappers hang
from the cafeteria ceiling;

no smoke curls
from *Girls.*

The gymnasium
is the same:

bulked-up players stream
from the locker room

into the glorious fall
apocalyptical

weather, where blue
and gold take the day.

# Lethe

## 1

To go back is to have forgotten
the names of the flowers,
though not their shapes and colors.
The hothouse words, spoken,
fall loose, unattached to any
blossom. Impatiens is just
impatience; embarrassment
is what I call the miniature
purple daisies that fold up at night,
even here, on my kitchen table.

## 2

And when the words come back they seem
all wrong, perverted, geranium
rhyming with cranium, or sounding
like Uranus. I bought one, coral
pink, having forgotten all of them
weren't red. Then your face surfaced
again, as if to rhyme, finally, with your name—
old garden tool, lost for a decade.
The tears surprised me, blurring the colors
somebody clipped and set in water.

# The Portrait of Your Ancestor

The lady doesn't live here anymore.
Only her pendant earrings, her pink wrap,
chocolate torrents of hair rolled into four
sausage curls, hands coupled above her lap;
her smile, which isn't yours; her burnt eyes
conveying a power that isn't yours, the seam
of her dress underlining her breasts, thighs
out of the picture, below the fat gold frame
that's been rubbed white in places, as if plied
with feathers or foam, although it's gilded wood.
The canvas, too, is wood: so heavy that
lowering it's like taking a square of wall
out of the wall—you need my help—but
miraculously the wall remains whole.

# A Girl Named Rose

Gifts were discouraged, but came anyway:
a scent, a scarf selected for its colors,
intensities of pink curled into flowers.
Dinner was salmon, and the wine, rosé.

A timeline, garnished with a red balloon,
held eighty years of life, but nothing more—
a job, a cruise. No marker for the war,
why she had never married, and how soon.

Money, longevity or tragic love:
she didn't seem to mind
what they were thinking of.
Under the apple tree, she cut the cake
into a million pieces, and the wind
took a napkin out into the lake.

# Rummage

In a thrift shop near Third,
I found the love I lost
sideways, by attrition,
a pair of pumps, barely worn,

and the imaginary child we abandoned.
I found your second wife
among the vintage dresses.
Together we tried on

your alligator wit and twirled
our fur-trimmed glee in it.
I found your wallet,
which smelled of mildew

with a hint of chocolate.
It was empty.
Where were your shirts, your shorts?
I suppose they didn't make the cut.

But I did find your chest—
the one with the glass knobs
and a little rusted wheel
locked underneath each foot.

It wasn't perfect,
but it still held that word
we all remember,
and the price was right.

III

# Emergency

3:20: when he fills the school bus door
and drops into light, dragging his orange pack,
I remember the tulips on Park Avenue,
like orange flames I waded through in labor
so heavy that I couldn't stand up straight.
Ages have passed since nurses laid him flat
on brown paper, and stretched him between two lines.
Floating on Percocet, I received in turn
each visitation and delivery:
the anxious brother, morphed as Superman,
a pyramid of fruit, a blue bouquet;
the father as Clark Kent, holding
a crimson spray like an emergency.
Now, when I take his hand and hoist his pack,
my winter eyes recoiling from the sun,
I remember, too, a red light impotent
to halt a river flow of poppy strobes
and sirens, neighbors huddled in singed air
as lines of fire engines headed south.
And how it felt impossible that we should be
still here, fully upright, untouched by fire,
crossing through islands of chrysanthemums.

# Thieves

Family jewels have ways of vanishing.
But the way your mother looked
when she poured them into your hands
will never disappear.

If she could still look at you
you would not tell her
how much became not yours
in this land of replaceable owners.

My father's father's watch, chain-dangled
under a bell jar of dust, long ago dropped
into insignificance in a pawn shop
of replicas, or melted down.

Who can distinguish life from things?
One night of weeping on the train to Queens.

# Lie

It starts like life, but skips over the F.
Then finishes, denying the omission

and holding firm, like any narrative
progressing from beginning to conclusion

across an opaque middle made of I.
A word composed of nothing except letters,

it rhymes with other words, like *my* and *die*.
It bears the weight of hope until it shatters

like thin ice, sharpness melting into sorrow.
One syllable, it can be made to grow

from the tongue's tip as long as breath can last,
or cut short with a sputter of disgust.

One word will do for what you didn't say
and what you did, no difference either way.

# Herbal

Startled to find a native variant
of what she'd started, the identical
gesture in miniature, she holds the plant
against its larger version: can she tell
the difference? Maybe. Has her seed escaped?
Doubtful, for now she sees them everywhere
outside the garden: lavender brush-shaped
clusters of wild heal-all, unplanned as air,
just like what's growing in her garden plot.
This is her question as she bends the book
open to where a specimen is shown
next to its healing uses: had she known
the thing as weed, would she have nurtured it?
Too late: it burgeons from the care she took.

# A Flemish Still Life

No effort's wasted if you aim to please.
Your pains are savored by the audience:
a flask of cabernet, a round of cheese.

The customer is charmed by what he sees
and what is meant. All flesh is decadence,
but nothing's wasted if you aim to please

with oysters, lemons, and a pair of these
boiled lobster claws like bloodied implements
framing the cabernet, the hunk of cheese,

the sweaty Muscats, and the peonies
swooning in leaded crystal. No expense
or effort's wasted when you aim to please

with spitted songbird, carved delicacies,
heaped quince on rumpled silk. Each day presents
another flask of wine, another cheese.
This paint is never wasted. Aim to please.

# American Cookery

> In all cakes where spices are named, it is supposed that
> they be powdered fine and sifted; sugar must be dried
> and rolled fine; flour dried in an oven; eggs well beat or
> whipped into a raging foam.
>
> Amelia Simmons, *American Cookery* (1796)

Made for "this country and all grades of life,"
my First Edition was not ridiculed
as was my station. Orphaned, neither wife
nor sister, a wage laborer, unschooled—
with only Character to call my own—
I made the most of little, learned to cook
from receipts that named not what was grown
hither; by their example, wrote this book
to teach the American Female methods and
ingredients known already in this land:
Indian corn, pearlash to raise a cake,
spruce beer and clams. My Second bred a fake,
printed in Boston with a lady's name.
Except to Him, the words are pressed the same.

# Looking for Silence

It's a kind of perfection, like death.
If you want it, maybe you want death.

There is nothing as silent as a classroom
just after a question has been asked.

Snow is a kind of silence
when you can't hear it falling

behind a plate glass window.
The fire snapping in a cool room

is not silence, but nostalgia
for it, almost the real thing.

A friend suddenly went deaf
in one ear. He was given silence

as penance for years of not listening,
according to his wife. It makes her sad

how half his life stalks him,
how he turns away to hear.

# The Walker

New thumping creature of bedtime
whose six legs include two

that are human: this heroine,
approaching the age of reason, is not

giving up, finally having achieved
a desired weightlessness, still living

alone, assisted by two housekeepers,
three daughters, and a telephone

stung by perpetual wrong numbers.
She would prefer her friends, their fingers hung

(fools that they are) with double diamonds.
Why tempt fate? She wears no jewels

tonight, keeps wondering why I'm here.
Though I *am* perfect, a darling. The light

must stay on in the bathroom.
Everything in its place. A fine dust

only where it cannot be removed:
across the bowls of strawflowers. Lonely

as Sancho Panza, I watch her pass
through rituals of net, cream and glass,

her metal horse knocking the sink.
Everything is perfect, only smaller.

Will *I* be warm enough? No time
to say before her sleeping pill

slips her from her mount and into
bed, between two plastic hips.

# Stagecraft

Colloid of stars deployed through atmosphere,
lowered in unison to staggered heights;
blue light on chiffon undulating waves,
the stark white faces lit by grief and age;
layers of curtains demarcating place
like skins of consciousness, like tissue paper
behind which pairs of skaters glide on ice,
before which ladies swoon across divans;
the rhythmic clanging of a lighthouse bell
(rain is the slanted light made visible)
a flash of silver on a lacquered trunk,
storm in the wings, the shipwreck understood.
Toast upon toast tipped into emptiness.
The fragrance of a burning cigarette.

# Sakura Park

At Riverside a flurry rides a gust
upward toward the pealing hour.
Yesterday the carillons rang sour.
Was it a joke or a beginner? Or just
a take on the cacophony of blather:

the year-end prattle of December
that fooled the new year into nothing better.
Those who believe in the letter
must still live by the number.
I found your suicide in the paper

though, in fact, I might have looked
out the window. I might have seen
silent catastrophe unlit by screen,
among windows pricked by lights, picked
out your black one underlined by snow.

Today I run on ice
softened by salt and rising temperatures.
I post another loss among our futures,
where even time will fall into the space
around your living words.

*Rachel Wetzsteon (1967-2009)*

# The Salamander's Castle

The salamander's castle
is large enough for him.
He has neither servants nor
family, no castle keeper.

Just a castle like bread
eaten through by worms
that he fills with himself.
From it one thick manly

leg protrudes. He has no
mate. His world is an eye
that only sees in, lit,
yet mired in its own dark

camouflage, a mud of leaves.
Rising up to kiss the surface,
he eats what he is given:
the clouds, the stars.

# Raising an Orchid

Although you didn't ask for it,
don't drown it. Keep it thirsty
and water it over the sink

so it can drain. Leave the roots
packed with strands of moss
in the pot that looks too small.

Mostly likely yours is sterile
and came with extra petals.
Enjoy them until they drop.

It will flower again when it wants to.
As many times as it wants to,
but rarely never.

Fertilizer helps and sun,
but not too much: a slant
of light and a rinse of water

to help it remember the rain
forest where it never lived
among the brilliant birds.

# Physical Therapy

Hold on for balance to the countertop.
Extend one leg behind and count to ten.
Lower it gently. Do not let it drop.

Repeat with other leg and do not stop.
You're stable as a bull in pasture when
you lean for balance on the countertop.

Stamina's growing like a bumper crop.
Muscles you thought you'd never use again
lower you gently, do not let you drop.

Soon you'll be dancing with the broom and mop
as habit sweeps you through the regimen.
Hold on for balance to the countertop

and rise above your toes like Jiffy Pop.
The rooster is the master of his pen.
Now lower gently. Don't let yourself drop.

Think Tommy Dorsey and the Lindy Hop.
Extend the arm of *now,* hold on with *then*
and shuffle us across the countertop.
Lower us gently. Do not let us drop.

# Task

The son performed the mother's funeral
the May after she died in February.
The mourners gathered in the cemetery,
filling a field that was already full
of dandelions. They spoke the usual.
He spoke into the wind, a blooming cherry
for introduction and the ordinary
shade trees for her life, a daffodil
for homily, a patch of onion grass
for shared amen, a mockingbird for sure,
a hawk for one who stood, silent, among
the others, vacant eyes obscured by glass,
and a rabbit for the son's son, whose song
I held to me, and so I couldn't hear.

# Wood Frogs

A dirge of words, our racket
stilled them. So now, we force
silence until they start again:
one scratch in the air and then another

until the air vibrates with sighs.
The first diagonal line
becomes a cross-hatched surface
of swimmers who collide and mount

each other, or get shaken off.
Haphazard love, trial and error,
will bring them, finally, to mate
and blur the surface with a cloud.

As song can hatch from icy water,
so legs will sprout for the dry season.
By June the clouds will sink
into the grass and we'll be gone.

# Song

The computer, the ice box, the knot of pipe
under the sink the relay the compressor
the trap the memory the piece of tape
the leak of grease the puddle of water

the warm heart of thawed death
the cave that can't preserve it
the corrupted registry, the unknown path
the escape backed up with shit

the conduit the wire the clicking sound
the virus, the worm, the wait and see
of the patch, the part the workaround
the short the overload the terminology

of impasse, inaction and malfunction
composed of words that can't be broken.

# Quilts: A Story

*Work in a series,* quoted the quilter
(her dead friend's advice) to the assembled.
Flowers or animals or chemicals,
the jumbled colors of another day
in the garden, primaries of midsummer.
Work in a series and you'll find you have
a better chance to finish what you've started.
Another child who is completely different.
Or another day to gather up the pieces
and clean the abandoned studio.

Relocating the family, remembered a son:
moving from one post to another
like scraps of fabric on a field of blue
tablecloth, from base to base into a new
country, an American breakfast. Home
again, she made it home, quilting a room
for each of them, avoiding triangles
and squares, choosing instead green
waves or purple bunches stitched
onto crossed diagonals like long arms

of blooming cherry. As for the husband,
the hobby she embraced to fill his absence
gave him the panels that contained his life:
furious flowers framed by days and years,
houses and holidays, the months at sea,

bright puffy cells dividing on a screen,
an empty garden filling up with rain.
Finally, learning how to wait together
became another perfect segment sewn
into a brilliant quilt that was not warm.

After, an emptiness that fails to move
beyond the pattern of familiar squares,
triangles and diamonds, a formal stew
whose expedient patchwork still demands
symmetry—a makeshift solace born
when an uncut measurement of cotton
was precious, not to be wasted on beds.
After, the daughter, holding her own
two children as if lost at sea, draped
in new pieces of old garments arranged

to repeat inseparably without a center.
The broken heart: yes, we know that quilt,
worked in a series, over and over.
It is made from pieces of potato sack
and new velvet, thrift and squander,
life and death, time within a border,
which, used, eventually will disappear, washed
into nothing, all work dismantling,
a pink rag waving against the blue sky,
pale flag of surrender, of having been.

## These Lines Are Beams of Light

These lines are beams of light or vice versa,
easily retracted or retraced en route.
I break them where I please with no eraser
or white-out. A kind of paint, white-out,

that comes in different shades to match
the paper. But words don't meet the paper
as often anymore. Words don't touch
the bed they lie above. Remember

what they used to say about our dancing?
They dance without touching! How
radical. Yet, inside, everyone was touching.
That's why I wonder if our words know

restlessness, even desire, as they move
from matter to ghostliness, having sublet
their bodies. And what would they love
if they could, our words? Not us, but

each other, those incestuous ghosts.
Once imprisoned on paper, now
they appear and disappear without pasts
or futures, barely remembering those who

release them into the ether, like smoke.
Still, they tell us what we're about
by yielding to the motions that we make
and leave politely when the light goes out.

# Return

Daybreak at the feeder:
a bulb of sugar water
where two friends hover,
now enemies—move over—
and twin engines sputter.

A pick-up wades the hill
where mud slips like butter.
What isn't weighted down
with last night's rain?
Just this iridescent

skirmish carrying the eye
upward on a dark day,
two warriors unleashed
from tapestry and book plate:
twin spirits lashed

as one, like love and sorrow,
against a wet tangle
of branches, whose radium fur
grows visibly each hour
in fog-sifted sun.

Ellen Kaufman earned an A.B. in English and Asian Studies from Cornell University, and M.S.L.S. and M.F.A. degrees from Columbia. Her poems have appeared in *Beloit Poetry Journal, Carolina Quarterly, The New Yorker, Poetry Northwest, Pool, Salamander, Seneca Review, Shenandoah, Southwest Review, Tar River Poetry, Think Journal,* and *Verse.* She has reviewed poetry for *Library Journal* since 1991. She was a 2009 MacDowell Colony

Fellow and won the *Southwest Review*'s 2012 Morton Marr Poetry Prize. *House Music* was a finalist for the 2012 Able Muse Book Award.

The mother of two grown sons, Kaufman lives with her husband in New York City, where she has worked as a law librarian and as a reference librarian for Baruch College.

## ALSO FROM ABLE MUSE PRESS

Ben Berman, *Strange Borderlands - Poems*

Michael Cantor, *Life in the Second Circle - Poems*

Catherine Chandler, *Lines of Flight - Poems*

Maryann Corbett, *Credo for the Checkout Line in Winter - Poems*

Margaret Ann Griffiths, *Grasshopper - The Poetry of M A Griffiths*

Carol Light, *Heaven from Steam - Poems*

April Lindner, *This Bed Our Bodies Shaped - Poems*

Frank Osen, *Virtue, Big as Sin - Poems*

Alexander Pepple (Editor), *Able Muse Anthology*

Alexander Pepple (Editor), *Able Muse - a review of poetry, prose & art*
   (semiannual issues, Winter 2010 onward)

James Pollock, *Sailing to Babylon - Poems*

Aaron Poochigian, *The Cosmic Purr - Poems*

Stephen Scaer, *Pumpkin Chucking - Poems*

Hollis Seamon, *Corporeality - Stories*

Matthew Buckley Smith, *Dirge for an Imaginary World - Poems*

Barbara Ellen Sorensen, *Compositions of the Dead Playing Flutes - Poems*

Wendy Videlock, *The Dark Gnu and Other Poems*

Wendy Videlock, *Nevertheless - Poems*

Richard Wakefield, *A Vertical Mile - Poems*


www.ablemusepress.com

CPSIA information can be obtained at www.ICGtesting.com
Printed in the USA
BVOW04s0721170714

358969BV00008B/36/P